Choosing the Right Cruise for You

- EASY-TO-READ
- TIME and MONEY-SAVING TIPS
- FIRST-TIME and REPEAT CRUISERS

John Wm. Macchi and Art Kane
Illustrations by: Jill Pabich

A BON VOYAGE GUIDE

CHOOSING THE RIGHT CRUISE FOR YOU
A Bon Voyage Guide
By John Wm. Macchi & Art Kane
Copyright © 1994 by John Wm. Macchi & Art Kane

Published by Distinctive Publishing Corp.
P.O. Box 17868
Plantation, Florida 33318-7868
Printed in the United States of America

Illustrations by Jill Pabich.

All rights reserved. No part of this book may be reproduced, stored in a retrieval system, or transmitted, in any form or by any means, electronic, mechanical, photocopying, recording or otherwise, without written permission of the publisher.

ISBN: 0-942963-52-0
Library of Congress No.: 94-29665
Price: $ 9.95

Library of Congress Cataloging-in-Publication Data

Macchi, John Wm. (John William), 1941-
      Choosing the right cruise for you : easy-to-read, time and money savings tips, first-time and repeat cruisers / John Wm. Macchi and Art Kane; ilustrations by Jill Pabich.

    p. cm.
"A Bon voyage guide."
Includes index.
ISBN 0-942963-52-0 : $ 9.95
1. Ocean travel. 2. Ocean ships. I. Kane, Art. II.Title.
G550.M15   1994
910.4'5--dc20   94-29665
                                        CIP

We would like to thank the following people who helped make this book possible:

Special thanks to John's wife, Patti, for her support and encouragement never to give up on an idea and a belief; and to Art's wife, Pauline, for her endless reviews and hours of editing and moral support.

Our thanks and gratitude to Debbie Adams for her encouragements that this was a book that should be written and her contribution in writing our Foreword.

Thanks to Midge Mills for her advice and suggestions in keeping the information both realistic for all cruise travelers.

And a tip-of-the-hat to Charles Grimley, our St. Louis connection, for his long-distance final editing but most importantly, for his long-term friendship.

J.M. and A.K.

TABLE OF CONTENTS

FOREWORD ii

I	CHOOSING YOUR FIRST CRUISE	1
II	MAKING YOUR CRUISE RESERVATIONS	11
III	TYPES OF CABINS	21
IV	FROM YOUR HOME TO YOUR CABIN	27
V	TAKING A TOUR OF THE SHIP	41
VI	THE DINING ROOM	51
VII	ACTIVITIES ON BOARD	65
VIII	PORTS OF CALL	75
IX	PRACTICAL ADVICE	79

APPENDIX:

I	CHECKLIST OF THINGS TO BRING WITH YOU ...	80
II	A CRUISE VOCABULARY	81
III	LIST OF CURRENT CRUISE SHIPS	83

FOREWORD

It seems that the pressures and stress of everyday life increase each year, making our vacation time more valuable than ever before. The quality of the choices we make in the spending of that time determine its success. That is what this book is all about.

Cruising has long conjured up images of romance, exotic ports of call and pampering. But when it comes to choosing your cruise, you discover that the choices are many and varied. Which is best for me? Where do I want to go? What should I pay? Should I use a travel agent? What is it really like on board a ship? The answer to these questions, and more, help to make the right decision to start your best vacation ever — your cruise vacation.

There are ships of all sizes, sailing to everywhere around the globe and offering different experiences. The services of your professional travel or cruise agent are invaluable in determining which is right for you. BUT...this book is the primer to prepare you to help them make the selection that best fits you.

I applaud your choice of a cruise vacation. You won't be sorry. As importantly, I applaud your choice of this book. It will help you guarantee that your cruise becomes your most exciting and memorable vacation ever.

Bon Voyage!

Debbie R. Adams
Past President
NACOA (National Association of Cruise Only Agencies)

INTRODUCTION

The information in this book is designed to help make you as comfortable as possible before you take your first cruise. In fact, it is a good guide for those who have cruised before and still have unanswered questions.

Cruise choices can overwhelm you. The number of ships and itineraries continue to grow each year. Talking to friends who have cruised before can only add to your confusion. Everyone has his or her own opinions.

And talk is cheap.

Having worked in the cruise industry for over fifteen years, we felt that the time was right to share our experiences in an easy-to-read guide that will answer the most commonly asked questions about the total cruise experience.

We do not cover every aspect of cruising. However, what we have covered in this book will give you useful information about taking your first cruise. We believe that experienced cruisers will find it helpful as well.

If we have missed an area that is of interest to you, let us know (There is a form in the back of this book for you to fill out), and we may include it in a future edition.

With the dynamics of the cruise industry today, we simply cannot cover every cruise line, every ship, every itinerary, and every individual way of doing business on the high seas. It is not the intention of this book. We want to tell you, in straightforward language, what a cruise is all about, how to reserve one, and what to expect once on board.

If this information helps to make your cruise experience more pleasurable, then our efforts have been rewarded.

See you on board.

John Macchi and Art Kane
Miami, Florida

1

CHOOSING YOUR FIRST CRUISE

So you're going to take a cruise!

Congratulations! What a smart choice you've made.

Well, now that you've decided to take that first, long-awaited cruise, perhaps you should sit down and ask yourself a few very important questions such as:

> WHERE WOULD YOU LIKE TO GO?
> FOR HOW LONG?
> WHEN CAN YOU FIND THE TIME TO TAKE A TRIP?
> WHO WILL SAIL WITH YOU?

And perhaps the most important question...

> WHY ARE YOU GOING?

Is it so that you can relax? Or are you looking to let your hair down and have a wild time? Do you want to visit a lot of ports? Or will you simply lie out by the pool while the ship sails smoothly at sea?

Only you can answer these questions.

This Guide will help you to look at the options available before you make the final decision on which cruise to choose.

2/CHOOSING THE RIGHT CRUISE FOR YOU

Let's take one question at a time.

We'll ask you the question, and you can write in your answer.

WHERE TO?

Most ships sailing from U.S. ports sail to 6 main geographical areas:

- THE CARIBBEAN
- MEXICO
- HAWAII
- ALASKA
- BERMUDA
- NEW ENGLAND

1.) I WOULD LIKE TO SAIL TO_____.
Turn to Chapter 8 and see the breakdown of ports and the season of the year for each sailing.

FOR HOW LONG?
The most common cruise itineraries are for 3, 4, and 7 days. You'll also find cruises that last 1, 2, 5, 10 days and longer.

I suppose if you look hard enough you can find a cruise somewhere in the world that will last as long as you want it to. Yes, around the world in 80 days (and longer) still exists!

2.) I THINK THAT A_____DAY CRUISE IS THE BEST FOR ME.

TIP: Cruises lasting 7 days offer the widest choice of itinerary selection.

WHEN CAN YOU GO?

You can usually find a cruise itinerary that will fit your time schedule if you plan to take your cruise between May and October. That's when all of the six geographical areas are open to cruising. It's also the busiest time of the year because that's when school is out and families take vacations.

When October arrives, Alaska and New England cruises phase out and more ships return to the Caribbean. So, October through May gives you the widest choice of Caribbean cruises.

Keep in mind the dates for school holiday vacations around Thanksgiving, Christmas, and New Year's can be sold out in advance. So plan early!

3.) I WANT TO SAIL DURING THE MONTH OF_____.

4.) THE BEST WEEK WILL BE_____.

5.) AN ALTERNATE WEEK WOULD BE_____.

WHO IS GOING WITH YOU, AND WHY?

Are you planning this cruise as a honeymoon?

A second honeymoon?

Or maybe a quick get-away for a weekend of relaxation for you and your spouse... or for you alone.

No telephones, a good book and lots of mid-day naps.

Is this the summer vacation family week of fun in the sun with the kids?

Or a wild run-as-fast-as-you-can week through the islands, sightseeing and shopping for bargains?

Whom you take will determine whether you need one cabin or two.
(We will discuss cabin accommodations in chapter 3.)

Just remember that some cabins can accommodate up to 4 passengers in upper and lower beds. Other cabins can offer queen-size beds. It all depends on your needs.

6.) THIS IS A CRUISE VACATION FOR ME AND_____.

SHIP SIZE

Size will usually determine the number of people you'll have onboard with you. Look at it this way and decide:

A Mega Ship = over 1800 people. This is truly a floating resort with a vast variety of activities, top quality entertainment from stage shows to intimate lounge acts to not-so-intimate discos. These fantastic ships offer elaborate casinos with a multitude of gaming activities as well as specialty lounges that serve only wine and champagne (a nice touch on formal night). At present there are seven mega ships in operation with plans to increase that number to 10 or 12. You can expect some crowding in the smaller ports when these ships arrive.

A Large Ship = over 1,200 people. It has many of the amenities of the Mega Ship without the added size and number of passengers. Average-priced cabins can be fairly uniform and quite comfortable, but tend to be on the small side. The large ships have more and larger public areas than smaller ships and this fact keeps them from appearing crowded. They usually have a broader variety of entertainment such as Broadway and Las Vegas type shows. Look for large casinos, lots of shops, and lots of people too.

A Medium Ship = 600 to 1200 people. These ships have average-priced cabins that are uniform and on many ships tend to be small. They are more intimate in design but roomy enough to spread out. They will give you many of the amenities of the large ship with a lot less people to run into. It's easier to get from one place to another without getting lost, and most public areas are within easy access. This size ship provides smaller crowds of people in the ports of call.

A Small Ship = Under 600 people. Average-priced cabins usually cost more but tend to be roomier and provide you with more amenities. You will find more intimate surroundings, usually elegantly appointed. There tends to be limited activities and entertainment compared to the larger ships. You will find that it's easy to meet or avoid people as you wish on a ship of this size. Remember, the smallest ships have the ability to sail into smaller, more exotic ports.

Cabin space is relevant. What is spacious to one traveler is small to another. Use the above information as a guide and not a hard and fast rule.

7.) I PREFER A:
MEGA___LARGE___MEDIUM___SMALL___SHIP.

OLDER SHIP vs NEW SHIP?

Both seem to have their advantages.

Older ships (built before 1970) usually have larger cabins, bathtubs with showers, lots of brass and wood, traditional port holes in outside cabins, and some even still have movie theaters to watch an afternoon film.

Newer ships (built after 1980) tend to provide smaller cabins, have showers, lots of stainless steel and glass, windows rather than port holes in outside cabins and televisions in the cabins where you lie in bed and watch the morning, afternoon, evening, or late-night movie.

Actually, once you're on board and having the time of your life, you won't care when the ship was built. We strongly suggest that you make your decision based on the itinerary and best value you can get for your money.

**8.) I DON'T CARE — I WANT A/AN:
OLDER ___ NEWER ___ SHIP.**

THEME CRUISES

Many of the cruise lines seem to be doing it. They are carrying a major theme onboard that appeals to certain tastes.

In recent years we've seen: '50s Rock n' Roll, Country and Western, Jazz, Sports Legends, Singing Greats, Golf, St. Patrick's Day, Alternative Lifestyles, Religious Groups, Academic, Scientific, Political and World Leaders, Authors — the list is endless.

If a theme cruise strikes your fancy, check with your Travel Agent Cruise Consultant for information on upcoming onboard events.

9.) **I'D REALLY ENJOY A CRUISE WITH A _____ THEME.**

MANY PORTS or MORE SEA TIME?

Now, based on what you've decided so far, you can pretty well determine exactly the kind of cruise you'd enjoy.

Do you want to visit a different port each day — 4 to 5 ports during a 7-day cruise with lots of sightseeing and shopping at different destinations?

Or do you prefer a more relaxed voyage — long lazy days at sea with more time to enjoy the ocean with limited visits to 2 or 3 ports during the 7 days on board?

A point to remember — there is little choice on the number of ports on a 3- or 4- day cruise. The limited time allows for a limited number of visits — usually one or two ports.

10.) **I VOTE FOR:**
MANY PORTS _____ MORE SEA TIME _____ .

ACTIVE OR QUIET?

There are some ships that sell lots of fun-in-the-sun and non-stop activities for young and old alike. On some of the larger ships, it seems that there is always something going on at all hours of the day, sometimes two and three activities at once; take your pick.

Other ships tend to offer a more relaxed pace, slow and steady. There are not a lot of activities to disturb your quiet nap by the pool, or that new novel you're reading in the comfortable lounge. It all depends on what you're looking for.

11.) FOR ME MAKE IT:
   ACTIVE _____ (Yahoo!) **QUIET** _____ (Ahhh...)

OK, you've just made the most difficult decisions regarding your cruise. Let's summarize those decisions:

1. I WOULD LIKE TO SAIL TO: _____.
2. I THINK THAT A ___ DAY CRUISE IS THE BEST FOR ME.
3. I WANT TO SAIL DURING THE MONTH OF _____.
4. THE BEST WEEK WILL BE: _____ _____.
5. AN ALTERNATE WEEK WOULD BE: _____.
6. THIS IS A CRUISE VACATION FOR ME AND _____.
7. I PREFER TO SAIL ON A _____ SIZE SHIP.
8. I PREFER A(N) _____ AGE SHIP.
9. I'D REALLY ENJOY A CRUISE WITH A _____ THEME.
10. I PREFER A CRUISE THAT VISITS MANY PORTS WITH LESS SEA TIME _____. I PREFER A CRUISE THAT VISITS FEWER PORTS WITH MORE SEA TIME _____.
11. I WANT A CRUISE THAT IS FUN-FILLED/ACTIVE _____. I WANT A CRUISE THAT IS RELAXED AND QUIET _____.

YOU NOW HAVE SOLID INFORMATION TO USE IN DECIDING WHICH CRUISE TO TAKE. LET'S FIND THE EASIEST WAY TO RESERVE YOUR CABIN AND GET YOU ON YOUR WAY TO THE HIGH SEAS!

2

MAKING YOUR CRUISE RESERVATIONS

Now that you've made up your mind to take your first cruise, how should you go about making your reservations? Be smart and take the best way which is also the easiest way: Call a good Travel or Cruise Agent.

WHY SHOULD I USE A TRAVEL OR CRUISE AGENT?

For simple reasons: They understand travel, they employ someone who knows about cruise lines and cruising, and they're FREE!

Yes, it's true; you don't pay for the travel agent's services; the cruise line pays them a commission on the cruise they book for you.

HOW SHOULD I CHOOSE A TRAVEL AGENCY?

Check the travel section of your Sunday newspaper and you'll find a good selection of agencies advertising cruises. The Yellow Pages is another option; as is word-of-mouth.

We suggest that you choose an agency which specializes in selling cruises, one that is an accredited member of the Cruise Line International Association (C.L.I.A.) and which is generally a member of the National Association of Cruise Only Agencies (N.A.C.O.A.).

WHAT SHOULD I EXPECT FROM THESE SPECIALISTS?

These agencies will have Cruise Consultants who have in-depth knowledge of all major cruise lines sailing from U.S. ports. These professionals are well trained in helping you to choose a cruise itinerary and will be able to identify the cruise line and ship that will match your needs.

The Cruise Consultant will provide you with the proper brochures and show you a video of the ships he or she recommends in order to help you become more comfortable with your selection. The consultant may also access the various cruise reservation networks by computer in order to find the best available cabin in your price range.

> *TIP: Call it a ship, not a boat!*

CAN I RESERVE MY CRUISE DIRECTLY WITH THE CRUISE LINE?

Sure you can but we don't advise it.

You'll find yourself calling a number of cruise lines in order to get all the information you need to make a sound decision. Many cruise lines prefer that you go through a travel agency in order to obtain the cruise information you need. And the agency is set up to deal directly with the traveler.

No one cruise line can answer all of your questions as well as your local cruise agency can. And because they are local, they can advise you on which airline flights the cruise line uses to fly you from your city to the ship.

If you're driving, they can advise you of the best route to take and all about parking at the port. It is just easier to use the cruise consultant at your local travel agency. And the price is right: it's free!

FARES—WHAT SHOULD I EXPECT TO PAY?

Like everything we buy, prices can fluctuate and, if we look around long enough, we can usually find a good deal; not always but most of the time. It's the same with cruises. Some seasons are less expensive than others.

Most cruise lines set their fares around 3 seasons (each may describe them in different terms) which we will call PEAK, OFF PEAK, and VALUE.

Think about the sales on bathing suits in New York at the end of the summer. You won't find these sales in Miami. The same holds true with cruises. The price fluctuates with the season and the demand for cabins on the ships.

Remember, though, to shop for value, not price. Cruise experiences do vary, and some may not be best for you, regardless of the price. Your travel or cruise agent can help you find the cruise vacation that is right for you at the best price. That's value!

CAN I GET A DISCOUNT ON MY CRUISE?

Usually. Unless you're making your reservation the day before you plan to sail during the height of the peak season, you can usually find a price break for the kind of cruise you want to take.

Always ask your cruise consultant to explore the availability of discounts for the time period you want to cruise. If you do your homework and ask a lot of questions regarding cabin availability on ships that fit your travel requirements, you will usually find a good value.

Early booking discounts, two-for-one cabins and cabin upgrades are usually available on most lines during the year.

One rule of thumb is that the farther in advance you book your cruise, the wider the range of discounts and ship choices you will find.

> *TIP: Ask if the Travel Agency you plan to use has blocked any cabins on a ship that fits your needs and itinerary. If the agency has, you may be able to get a better price on what would be equivalent to a Group Rate.*

WHAT IS A GROUP RATE ?

It's a special rate, usually discounted, for people who take the cruise with a group of friends rather than as a couple or small family. You need a minimum of 10-16 people to form a group; it depends on the cruise line.

Your group can represent anything you want: family reunion, bowling league, church group, etc. as long as they all make the reservation together as a group.

Some cruise consultants can arrange for the people in your group to sit in the same part of the dining room, enjoy a private cocktail party, and provide other amenities that make the cruise a special occasion. Group rates are lower than individual rates.

WHAT IS AN AIR/SEA PACKAGE ?

Since 1982, cruise lines have generally included air fare in the price of the cruise. It is called an Air/Sea package.

Your cruise reservation automatically makes an airline reservation from your home city to the port city, and back home again. The cruise line purchases these airline tickets at special volume rates, which are usually much less expensive than you would pay on your own. It also includes transfers for you and your baggage to and from the airport and the pier.

You may prefer to make your air arrangements separately. You would then reserve your cruise on a cruise only basis (see next topic). Be aware that when you do not purchase the air/sea package, the cruise line does not furnish the transfers. Your travel or cruise agent can advise you on the methods of transfer and approximate cost from the airport to the ship.

You should also know that when you purchase an air/sea package, the cruise line chooses the airline and routing you will use from allotments given to them by the airlines. If you want to be guaranteed a certain airline or route, you may want to reserve your cruise on a cruise only basis and buy your air separately.

WHAT IS A CRUISE ONLY RATE?

Cruise lines also offer a less expensive Cruise Only rate for those who may prefer to drive to the ship's port of embarkation or for those who may be able to secure a cheaper air fare. That would make their total cruise price a lot less expensive.

Check with your cruise consultant for the current fares; you may find that an airline is offering a lower fare than the Air/Sea rate. If you decide to drive to the ship, remember that parking can cost from $5.00 to $20.00 a day.

Also remember that when traveling as an Air/Sea passenger, an additional benefit is that you will be met at the airport by a cruise representative, your baggage will be handled by the cruise line, and you will be transported directly to the ship, all at no additional charge! It is something to think about.

> **TIP:** *Insist that the Travel Agency guarantee to protect your discounted rate. In other words, if your cabin is offered at a lower price in the future, will the agency refund the difference? If you cancel your first reservation to take advantage of the lower fare, you may be charged with a cancellation penalty which could offset any savings on the lower rate. Ask the Travel Agent first!*

CAN I LEAVE A DAY EARLY OR STAY A DAY OR TWO AFTER THE CRUISE?

Why not? Sounds like a great idea if you have the time.

Most cruise lines have special sail-and-stay rates with hotels and resorts that let you enjoy the city you sail from and the surrounding areas either before you sail or following your cruise. These Pre-Cruise and Post-Cruise Packages are available for all U.S. ports as well as port cities in the Caribbean and Canada.

It is an easy and economical way to visit such cities as Miami, Ft. Lauderdale, Montego Bay, San Juan, Montreal, Vancouver, Los Angeles, San Diego and many more. It is also an economical way to visit family and friends who live near these port cities. Check with your cruise consultant for Pre- and Post-Cruise Specials.

WHAT ARE THESE PORT CHARGES I HAVE TO PAY?

Port charges are costs, not included in your cruise fare, that comprises port and federal taxes and special handling charges imposed by the port authority from where the ship sails and by the various ports visited on the cruise. They help to keep the ports in good condition, make necessary repairs to the docks, and maintain the facilities in general. Port charges are determined by the number of ports on your cruise. They can total up to $100.00 or more, per person. Your cruise consultant can tell you the total port charge you will pay for the cruise you choose.

WHEN DO I PAY FOR MY CRUISE? CAN I USE MY CREDIT CARD?

The easiest way is to write a check for the whole enchilada!

However, cruise lines will also take most major credit cards. Your cruise consultant will know which card each cruise line accepts.

You will be asked to pay a deposit or, in some cases, a minimum of 10% at the time you make your reservation. The balance is due at least 30 days before you sail. Some cruise lines require that you pay the balance 60 to 90 days prior to holiday sailings.

IF I CANCEL MY CRUISE, DO I RECEIVE A REFUND?

Yes, but it depends when you cancel. Most cruise lines require written notice of cancellation and will refund your payment in full if you cancel at least 30 days before the sailing date. Other cruise lines may require 60 days' notice for full refund. A cancellation fee is usually charged if you cancel less than 30/60 days before sailing. Check with your cruise consultant for the policy used by the cruise line that you choose.

WHAT HAPPENS IF I ARRIVE LATE AND MISS THE SHIP?

If you are flying to the ship on an Air/Sea Package and your flight is delayed or cancelled because of bad weather (which can happen during the winter months) the cruise line will generally hold the ship at the port for as long as possible until as many late arriving passengers arrive. However, the ship will not wait overnight.

If the ship has to sail without you, the cruise line will generally arrange to fly you, at its expense, to meet the ship at it's first port of call.

If you are flying (or driving) on your own and you miss the ship, then you will have to arrange to fly yourself, at your expense, to the next port of call. No refunds will be issued.

SHOULD I BUY TRIP CANCELLATION INSURANCE?

We think you should. It protects you from unforeseen problems beyond your control such as accident, illness, or other circumstances that would cause you to cancel the cruise.

Trip Cancellation Insurance (also called Trip Interruption Insurance) is moderately priced per person and sold on a flat rate per $100.00 of coverage. Many of the policies are comprehensive in that they cover trip cancellation, trip interruption, and travel delay. They cover you if you have to cancel your cruise because of injury or illness to you or a traveling companion, or an immediate family member. The policy should protect you from being charged a cancellation fee—as long as you provide written notice up to 24 hours prior to sailing. Many policies will cover you up to the last minute if you cancel. Check with your cruise consultant for the details about this insurance.

Whether you are purchasing Cruise Cancellation Insurance or Travel Delay Insurance, be sure to read the policy carefully. If you have questions, call the company issuing the policy for the answers. Remember, your travel agent or cruise consultant is not a licensed insurance agent and is not bound by any information they give you regarding this insurance.

HOW ABOUT INSURANCE ON MY LUGGAGE?

Again, we think it's a good idea to insure all of your baggage especially if you are traveling to the ship by air. The airline has limited responsibility for your baggage, and the cruise line has little to none at all.

We suggest that you first check your homeowners policy to see if it covers loss or damage to personal items when traveling. If you do not have a homeowners policy, check with your cruise consultant or insurance carrier for rates and availability of add-on riders that can be put on the basic trip cancellation policy.

TIP: One of the better values we have found is Safe Sail Travel Insurance, sold through NACOA. It is quite comprehensive covering trip concellation, interruption, missed connection, travel delay, medical emergency and transportation, baggage damage and delay and travel accident. This policy can be purchased for a flat rate for either an individual or family. Cost depends on the total cost of your cruise. And there is no deductible.

3

TYPES OF CABINS

Ever since the television show, *The Love Boat*, people have had the idea that cabins on cruise ships were as large as hotel suites. Actually, some really are, but they are the exceptions.

Most cabins on ships today, especially the newer ships, tend to be very economical in size. That's a polite way of saying that they are fairly compact! However, once on board you'll discover that you spend relatively little time in your cabin. The size becomes secondary to the overall experience of shipboard activities.

Here are a few points of information about your cabin you should know for your first cruise:

DOES CABIN LOCATION DETERMINE ITS PRICE?

Yes, it usually does.

Cabins are identified by category, and categories are determined by the location of the cabin on the ship, whether they are inside (no windows) or outside (with windows), in the middle of the ship (sometimes less ship motion) or situated to the front (sometimes more ship motion) or back of the ship (vicinity of the engines). Each category has a specific price.
- Outside cabins cost more than inside cabins.
- The higher the deck, the more the cabin will cost.

- Cabins located amidships (middle of the ship) will sometimes cost more.

> **TIP:** *Take care to ask your Cruise Consultant to check with the ship deck plan to determine if a public room is located directly above your cabin. Even though most modern cruise ships are sound insulated, on some it can be a problem trying to sleep in a cabin directly below the Disco or the Nightclub dance floor.*

WHAT FEATURES WILL MY CABIN HAVE?

Again, it will depend on the age of the ship.

Many of the older ships simply don't have all of the cabin features found on the newer ones. Remember, older ships usually have somewhat larger cabins. Regardless of age, all cabins have a private bathroom with shower.

Electrical outlets (usually one in the bathroom and one near the dressing table) are 110 volt U.S. standard, so you usually don't need to bring an electrical voltage converter or plug adaptors. These devices are necessary when traveling in Europe, South America and the Orient but not onboard most cruise ships sailing out of U.S. ports. Check with your Cruise Consultant about the need for converters based on the ship you choose.

Also, each cabin will have a television for onboard movies and ship-produced programs and a telephone for cabin-to-cabin communication.

Cabin furniture includes twin beds that may double as sofas during the day (some are capable of being positioned together to form a double bed); dresser and mirror; chair; closet with hangers; night tables; wall lights over the beds.

Depending on the age of the ship and the category of the cabin, you may find the following features in your cabin: digital alarm clocks; bathroom wall-attached hairdryers; bathtub; bidet; sofa and coffee table; lounge chairs and footstools; double or queen-size bed; satellite ship-to-shore telephone service (a convenient but still costly feature); video tape player, and more.

Most of the newer ships offer the convenience of in-cabin personal safes for your documents and valuables. This convenience eliminates having to tote your passport and valuables to the Purser's Desk for safe keeping. Some in-cabin safes use a combination lock; others use keys. If the key is not in the lock, your cabin steward will have it and will require you to sign for it. There is no fee for use of the safe; however, there is a charge for lost keys. Don't forget to return the key to its proper location when leaving the ship.

> *TIP: An outside cabin on a lower deck can be the same size as an outside cabin on a higher deck but will cost less and save you money.*

SHOULD I CONSIDER A SUITE?

First-time cruisers usually don't opt for the luxury (and added cost) of a suite.

However, we know seasoned travelers who will not sail any other way and are willing to budget accordingly in order to pay for the advantages of a suite.

The major differences in a suite is size. Suites are more spacious and have queen or king-sized beds; some have the choice of a balcony or sitting room. The bathroom is larger, usually with a full-sized bathtub, many with double sinks, bidet, and jacuzzi. Suites may come with an audio-visual center: T.V. and stereo; refrigerator; personal safe; complimentary bar service; magnificent decor and the knowledge that you have one of the best cabins on the ship.

Most often, suites are situated high in the ship and in quiet areas for maximum privacy.

> *TIP: Many of the newer ships now have Mini-Suites which are smaller versions of the full suite, with similar features and amenities at a lesser cost.*

CAN I RESERVE A CABIN FOR MYSELF ALONE?

Sure you can.

A lot of people travel alone and meet new friends on the cruise. You can reserve a single cabin for yourself alone at one and a half the regular fare. Some cruise lines have special single fares!

Or, you can allow the cruise line to choose another single person of your same sex who is sailing alone and put you both into a single cabin at the regular fare. This can be a good deal, especially if you are the only single traveling on that cruise; you get the cabin to yourself and save paying the additional 1/2 fare.

CAN I PUT A 3RD AND 4TH PERSON IN MY CABIN?

Many ships have cabins that will accommodate up to four people, using twin lower beds and twin upper beds (called berths). The third and fourth person in a cabin, whether adults or children, will pay a lower rate than the first two occupants.

Many families find it quite economical if they reserve a cabin for four and put the kids in the same cabin as themselves. It cuts down on privacy and makes for tight accommodations, but such reservatons can save a lot of money.

> *TIP: Most cruise lines have age limitations for children occupying a cabin of their own. Check with your Cruise Consultant for details before booking a separate room for the kids.*

ARE THERE CABINS FOR THE PHYSICALLY CHALLENGED?

All of the newer ships have cabin accommodations for the physically challenged.

These newer ships will have elevators; wider doorways; cabins located on decks that allow easy access to dining and shops; lower shelving in the cabins; safety bars in the bathroom; specially designed shower and toilet facilities in order to accommodate the physically challenged guest.

Many of the older ships have redesigned a number of cabins in order to accommodate those guests in wheelchairs and other physically challenged passengers.

> *TIP: Find out which deck is used for disembarking (getting off) the ship. This deck will usually be used to store passenger luggage the final night at sea before reaching home port. It can be difficult for the physically challenged to maneuver around the luggage. The best bet is to book a cabin on a different deck.*

4

FROM HOME TO YOUR CABIN

WHICH PERSONAL DOCUMENTS SHOULD I BRING?

If you have a valid passport, bring it along. Proof of citizenship is needed and a valid passport is desired.

If you don't have a passport or do not have time to order one, a birth certificate with a raised (embossed) seal will substitute for a passport for U.S. citizens only. All other nationalities should carry a valid passport.

> *TIP: Driver's license and voter's registration cards do not qualify as valid proof of citizenship.*

Take your driver's license for check-cashing purposes and identification when using credit cards ashore. Having a photo identification card is a good idea in case it is required.

CAN I USE MY CREDIT CARDS ONBOARD THE SHIP?

Yes. However many cruise lines prefer that you conform to their onboard credit system, which may differ somewhat from cruiseline to cruiseline.

Usually, you'll be asked to present one major credit card

when you check in at the pier. A cruise line representative will take an imprint of that card and present you with an on-board identification card that is used for boarding purposes and also for charging items to your cabin. Other cruise lines perform this function onboard the ship, at the information desk.

You seldom have to use cash from that point while onboard. All onboard charges will be made with your ship identification card. A total of these charges will be submitted in statement form and delivered to your cabin the last night of the cruise. All of these charges will automatically be billed to the credit card you presented at check-in.

> *TIP: Be sure to check which credit cards the cruise line will and will not accept. Some cruise lines will not accept certain credit cards for payment or for on board charges.*

WILL I NEED CASH ONBOARD THE SHIP?

Most ships today do not accept cash. Exceptions include the gift shop, casino gambling and for tipping.

Gift shop purchases can be charged to your cabin or paid by cash. So, other than buying your onboard gifts or sundries, the only time you will need cash is if you plan to gamble or to pay your gratuities at the end of the cruise (and occasional tips for any special services provided by the staff).

HOW ABOUT TRAVELERS' CHECKS?

They are still a safe bet to take with you. You won't have any problems cashing them on the ship at the Purser's Desk (Information Desk.)

WHAT CLOTHES SHOULD I PACK?

It all depends on where the ship is going.

For Alaska and New England you should pack a warm jacket, sweaters, turtlenecks, warm cotton socks, and good walking shoes. You really don't need to pack any unusual winter clothing.

If you should decide to take a helicopter trip onto the glaciers in Alaska, the cruise line will provide special clothing (parkas and boots) for the trip. Since you'll be ashore during the heat of the day and it will be during the summer months, it's a good idea to layer your clothes so that you can remove a layer as you feel the need to do so.

May and October will be the coolest months in both areas, and it can be downright cold outdoors at the glaciers in Alaska or whale-watching off the New England coast. Pack—but don't overpack.

The Caribbean, Mexico, Hawaii, and Bermuda call for shorts and comfortable light cotton outerwear.

Stay away from clothes made of polyester as they tend to be dreadfully warm in these climates. Stick to cotton shirts, slacks, shorts, and the like.

Good walking shoes or sturdy sandals are a good idea as is a comfortable hat. Don't forget sunglasses.

TIP: Pack a comfortable sweater or sweatshirt regardless of where you are cruising. You'll find that they come in handy in the dining room and other public rooms in the morning where the air-conditioning has been on all night.

WHAT SHOULD I WEAR DURING THE DAY WHILE ON BOARD?

Relax, you're on vacation. Dress for the climate. Be comfortable. During warm weather most men and women will wear shorts and T-shirts or short-sleeved collared shirts everywhere around the ship. Swimsuits are not acceptable indoors unless worn with a shirt, robe, or other covering. When having lunch in the dining room, proper, yet comfortable attire is a must.

WHAT IS BEST TO WEAR WHEN GOING ASHORE?

Again, dress for the weather.

Shorts or slacks and a comfortable shirt or sweater are customary.

In the warmer climates, you will see many shipboard travelers walking around town in shorts and a T-shirt bearing the name of the ship they are cruising on. Most young travelers tend to dress very casual when going ashore.

Wear good walking shoes as some of the sidewalks and streets in Mexico and the Caribbean can be treacherous underfoot. They also protect your feet for the dancing you'll do later that evening.

It's wise to wear sunglasses and a hat during the heat of the day in many ports during the summer (and winter) months, and applying a good sunscreen is always a wise decision. The ship's gift shop will carry the proper sunscreen for the ports you will visit.

> *TIP: More and more people are wearing zippered waistpacks to carry their valuables when shopping on shore. They not only can hold your money and other documents more securely, they tend to be more convenient and secure in areas where pickpockets prey on the tourists. You can buy them in the ship's gift shop.*

WHAT FORMAL CLOTHES WILL I NEED TO BRING WITH ME?

On most 7-day cruises you will have two formal nights.

One will be the night of the captain's cocktail party, and you will have the opportunity to meet the captain and have your photograph taken with him (as of this writing there are no female ship's captains on cruise ships sailing out of U.S. ports).

Men — Pack your tuxedo if you have one. You can wear it both nights and not feel out of place.

However, if you don't own a tuxedo, don't go to the expense of renting one unless the cruise line requires it (most do not) or you simply want an excuse to dress up. Bring a dark suit. Again, depending on the ship, you'll find between 40 to 60 per cent of the men wearing dark suits rather than tuxedos.

Some cruise lines will have a tuxedo rental service onboard. Average cost is $ 65 - $ 75. Very convenient for those who wish to dress formal yet not fuss with packing a tuxedo.

As last resort, bring a nice pair of grey slacks and a blue blazer.

Ladies — Don't make it complicated! Many women complain about not taking a cruise because they don't have the proper clothes to wear on formal nights.

You will discover that most women will wear a cocktail dress or other appropriate evening attire such as a dressy pants suit. Long dresses are acceptable but not necessary. We are seeing fewer long dresses on cruises. A cocktail-length dress will serve the purpose just as well. Forget ultra-formal long gowns such as you see at weddings. We don't seem to see many of them on a cruise. Be practical and comfortable.

> *TIP: On formal nights, it's nice to stay dressed in your formal attire even though many people want to rush back to their cabin and change into shorts and sport shirts. Don't do it! For these one or two evenings, it's a pleasure to look at nicely dressed people. Tuxedos and tanktops simply do not mix!!*

WILL THE SHIP HAVE A DOCTOR ON BOARD?

Yes, every ship must sail with a doctor and nurse on board.

Your ship will have a medical facility that is capable of handling routine emergencies only. Passengers are advised to bring all personal prescription medication with them as it will not be available on board the ship.

WILL I NEED ANY SHOTS OR VACCINATIONS?

Unless your personal physician recommends it, you will not require any precautionary booster shots prior to sailing in any of the six regions mentioned in this book.

CAN I BRING MY PETS?

Although a cruise line may permit it, bringing a pet is very rare and we advise not doing so. Most cruise ships don't have any special facilities for animals. Check with your cruise consultant before making any final decision to bring your pet.

WILL I BE MET AT THE AIRPORT WHEN I ARRIVE?

Yes, if the cruise line has made your air reservation, you'll be met upon arrival by a representative of the cruise line. He or she will be wearing some sort of uniform that will identify him or her as a cruise line employee. Some representatives carry a sign identifying the ship or cruise line. Depending upon the airport regulations, the representative may be at the gate when you arrive; in the lobby; or in the baggage claim area.

HOW WILL I GET TO THE SHIP?

The cruise line representative at the airport has a list of all arriving passengers who are sailing with that cruise line on an air/sea basis. This representative will assemble you in a group and escort you to a waiting bus or van which will take you directly to the ship.

In some cases, passengers reserving a suite are met by chauffeured limousine service.

If you made your own travel arrangements, you will find convenient taxi service to the ship at all airports.

WHAT HAPPENS TO MY LUGGAGE?

No problem! If you are flying on a cruise line air ticket, your luggage will be handled separately by the cruise line. The next time you see it, it will be on board the ship and inside your cabin.

If you are driving to the port, you can drop off your luggage with the porters at the pier entrance and they will see that it is delivered on board your ship.

CAN I CARRY IMPORTANT LUGGAGE WITH ME?

Yes, and it's a good idea to keep any personal items of importance with you at all times.

You can carry whatever you wish onto the ship. We recommend that you put anything that is easily breakable or items that you'll need immediately upon arrival on board the ship into your carry-on baggage.

> *TIP: Put baggage tags with your name and cabin number on all luggage — even those that you plan to carry — in case you finally decide to have it sent on board by the porters or you accidentally misplace it in the port terminal.*

WHAT CAN I EXPECT WHEN I ARRIVE AT THE PIER?

That depends on when you arrive.

Boarding begins around 1:00 P.M. for most evening (5 - 7 P.M.) sailings. That is the busiest time and the pier can be total pandemonium! Everyone wants to get on board, have lunch, and look around as soon as possible.

Unless dining room seating has been arranged beforehand, early arrivals have first opportunities to select their seating for dinner. If you are traveling with a group of friends and wish to sit together at main seating, arrive early and make your reservations with the Maitre d' or Dining Room Manager.

> *TIP: If dining room seating selection is not a priority, plan to arrive at the ship around 2:30 P.M. and you'll find fewer people, lines, and less confusion. Since most ships serve lunch until 3:30 or 4:00 P.M., you should have plenty of time to eat and look around and reserve your seating for dining.*

IF I DROP OFF MY LUGGAGE, HOW MUCH SHOULD I TIP THE PORTERS?

The porters are employees of the port and not the cruise line. They are responsible for getting your luggage onto the ship. If the cruise line transported your luggage separately, you need not tip. However, if you drive and a porter carries your luggage from your vehicle, you should tip that porter personally.

The rule of thumb today is 75¢ to $1.00 per bag, depending on how many you have.

Always tip to ensure that your luggage arrives at the correct ship in good condition!

WILL I HAVE TO FILL OUT ANY DOCUMENTS?

Just a few. The cruise line will need information for immigration, onboard credit, the name, address and telephone number of a person to be contacted in case of emergency. Know your Social Security number, and have your passport or other photo identification with you.

> *TIP: Ask if your Cruise Consultant can arrange for all documents that must be filled out prior to boarding the ship be included in the envelope with your tickets and baggage tags. It will save you the time and inconvenience of having to complete them at the pier when you are anxious to board the ship.*

WHAT HAPPENS WHEN I CHECK IN AT THE PIER?

A representative of the cruise line will examine your tickets and immigration documents, take an impression of the major credit card you wish to have items charged to while on board, give you your dining room seating assignment and your dining time (unless the ship has open seating for evening meals), and provide you with a boarding pass for you and each person traveling with you.

Some cruise lines wait until you are on board before asking for an impression of your credit card.

You may be asked to present identification in the form of a passport or Birth Certificate to insure that you have it with you.

WHAT'S A BOARDING PASS?

The boarding pass is a card that proves you are a passenger on that particular ship.

You are required to show it to a crew member each time you board. The boarding pass may also double as your on-board charge card for payment of beverages and other items purchased during the cruise.

Many newer ships employing a keyless cabin entry system use the boarding pass as your cabin key as well.

WHERE'S THE PHOTOGRAPHER?

Unless you arrive close to the sailing hour, the photographer is usually ready to photograph you and those traveling with you just before you enter the ship. This, and other photos taken during the cruise, both formal and informal, are displayed in the photo gallery and are available for purchase throughout the cruise. Ample information about photographs is available on board.

> *TIP: Buy your photographs each day rather than wait until the end of the cruise. Because of the sheer volume of photographs taken during a cruise, photographs are removed from the gallery viewing board and placed into a file. It can be very time-consuming trying to find a special photo again, especially during the final-night crunch of last-minute photo-buying.*

WHAT HAPPENS WHEN I STEP ON BOARD?

Get ready to receive great service from the moment you step onto the ship. It's like stepping into a different world.

You'll be met by members of the ship's staff who are there to greet you, provide you with information, and answer any questions you may have. Stewards will then take any carry-on baggage you have and escort you to your cabin.

> *TIP: Even though the ship is mostly a cashless society, you will be expected to pay all gratuties (tips) in cash except for those that are automatically added to your bar bills. (See section on Tipping)*

CAN I INVITE VISITORS ON BOARD?

Usually not.

International security regulations instituted in recent years prevent you from inviting anyone who is not sailing to join you on board for a bon voyage party or to visit your cabin. Some cruise lines occasionally make exceptions to this rule provided that you arrange for the visitors in advance. However, in recent years more and more cruise lines are drawing the line dramatically and holding firm to their no visitor policy including immediate family members who are not sailing.

No cruise line will allow visitors on board who are not official guests of the cruise line or guests of ticket-holding passengers.

WHO IS A CABIN STEWARD/STEWARDESS?

This is the person who is responsible for keeping your cabin in immaculate condition. Your cabin steward may be a stewardess.

Most cruise lines employ men for this position although more and more are now hiring women, especially in the higher category cabins and suites.

Your cabin steward will magically appear at your cabin door soon after you arrive. He or she will introduce himself or herself to you, check your name against their rooming list, determine whether you are on first or second seating for dinner (so they can make up your bed while you eat), explain the details of the cabin to you (television, safe, etc.) and ask if you need anything for the cabin (extra blankets, pillows, beds put together as a double, etc.).

Usually, the next time you'll see your cabin steward is when you are leaving for meals. Somehow, they manage to enter your cabin and perform miracles when you are not around.

TIP: If you are used to sleeping in a double bed, many cabins with single beds can be arranged in a double-bed format. Ask your cabin steward if he or she can pull the beds together. You'll find the arrangement quite comfortable.

IS THERE REALLY A LIFE BOAT DRILL?

There sure is! And we suggest that you attend.

It's really a U.S. Coast Guard regulation for all cruise ships sailing from U.S. ports to have an organized life boat drill prior to the ship entering open waters. The drill takes about 1/2 hour and is a good, lively way to meet your new travel companions while being instructed on where to find your muster station (your lifeboat location) and what to do in case of an emergency.

Don't take the drill lightly; it is quite important. Anyway, all ship's services (and the bars) close for the duration of the drill, so it's just as well that you attend.

Look for the photographer, too!

5

TAKING A TOUR OF THE SHIP

By the time the Life Boat Drill has ended, the ship should be just about ready to sail or, in fact, be underway. Now is the perfect time to take a tour of the ship and get acquainted with the various public rooms and understand how each department works together in order to make your cruise the magical experience that it will become.

WHERE DO I BEGIN?

Wherever you wish.

This book will introduce you to each department so that you'll have a better understanding of the responsibilities of each when you take your ship tour for real.

Some folks start at the information desk and tour up to the pool and sun deck. Others do the reverse. So, purchase a cool drink and start strolling throughout your new home away from home.

INFORMATION DESK

Some ships still call it the Purser's Desk but as cruise ships take on a hotel-like appearance, more of them refer to this department as the Front Desk or Information Desk.

This is where you get your questions answered, pick up various shipboard information, report any problems with your cabin, buy stamps, cash traveler's checks, leave or receive messages, etc.

It is the focal point of the ship for information similar to the front desk in a hotel, except that you don't have to stop and register while on a cruise. That is all done beforehand on the pier.

You will find the Chief Purser or Front Desk Manager, Assistant Pursers or Informationists at the information desk, and they are all responsible to the Hotel Manager, the person responsible for all of the non-technical passenger services of the ship.

TOUR DESK

On the newer ships, this department may be located near the Information Desk.

It is responsible for handling all on-shore tours and trips offered by the cruise line. The Tour Manager (or Tour Director) will oversee all shoreside activities and can offer you both information and the ticketing for tours, shopping, shows, and day trips.

SHOW LOUNGES

There are usually two or more on each ship, one designed for large main shows and another for the more relaxing before- and after-dinner entertainment in more intimate surroundings. Many of the larger ships have multi-tiered lounges designed for full-scale Broadway productions. Other ships, mostly those that are smaller or older, have lounges designed for more cabaret-style entertainment.

THE DISCO

This is certainly of great importance to the younger cruiser. The disco is a hubbub of activity after 10 PM. Adorned with the usual array of lights and speakers, it offers a world of today's music and dance styles. Although fun to visit when it's in full swing, the Disco at night is definitely not the place for those who enjoy ballroom dancing and the big-band music of the '30s and '40s! The Disc Jockey (D.J.) runs tapes, records, and compact discs until the wee hours of the morning, usually 2:00 A.M.- 3:00 A.M. During the day and early evening, the Disco can be used for lectures, movies, or private parties.

MEETING ROOMS

They can be found on most newer ships, used for both social and business meetings. These rooms are designed to house audio and visual aids for lectures and comfortable seating with modular tables for ease of set up and meeting design. When not in use for meetings, the ship may open them up for relaxation, card games and the like. The Information Desk can give you more information on reserving a meeting room or arranging a small, private cocktail party.

BARS

Bars are located throughout the ship and are usually found in areas such as in or near the show lounge, the casino, and the swimming pool. Some ships will have special bars that cater to wines and champagnes exclusively. The outside pool bar allows for bathing attire to be worn at all times. Each bar will have one or more bartenders, bar or cocktail waiters and waitresses to serve you. The Bar Manager and Assistant Bar Manager are directly responsible for the bar operation. They, in turn, report to the Hotel Manager or the Food and Beverage Manager.

CASINO

The casino is a favorite and exciting spot on every cruise ship—if only to watch other passengers play!

The casino has strict operating hours. It cannot open until the ship is at least 3 miles from shore. It must remain closed during the time the ship is in any port. Once on the high seas, the casino can be open from morning until the following morning!

On most ships the casino is a concession, owned and operated by a company under contract to the cruise line. As a result, the casino employees may not be direct employees of the cruise line.

On all ships you will find 25¢ and $1.00 slot machines (you may still find 5¢ and 10¢ slot machines on some ships, but they are rapidly disappearing), Black Jack (21), and some form of Stud Poker (Caribbean Poker) tables. Many ships also offer Roulette, Craps, Dollar Wheels, Computer Horseracing and other games of chance, depending on the size of the casino. The casino croupiers (dealers) report to the Casino Manager. Remember, you must be at least 18 years old to enter the casino. No children, please!

More cruise lines are imposing stricter rules regarding young children in the casinos or playing the slot machines with parents. It is a good rule to encourage children to utilize the video game room designed exclusively for them.

GIFT SHOPS

The onboard shops are also usually a concession and not owned by the cruise line.

Gift shop personnel, usually not employees of the cruise line, report to a Gift Shop Manager. Depending on available space, the gift shops can be segmented to handle only one type of item (perfume, women's clothing, beach attire, logo attire, sundries, perfume and liquor, jewelry, etc). Many of the newer and larger ships have the shops arranged in a cluster on one deck for ease of shopping. The older and smaller ships may have one shop selling a multitude of items.

Look for the special sales (cut stones, men's and women's watches, rings, jewelry and gold by the inch, etc.). You can get some very good buys.

> *TIP: Always check the prices on board before making the final decision to buy at a shop on shore. Many times the onboard prices are the same or lower, especially on designer brands of purses and watches and some brands of liquor.*

Before arriving at each port, there will be a lecture on the historical and geographical sites of interest. However, the port lecturer will often make suggestions on which stores to shop during your visit shoreside. You should know that many of these shops pay a promotional fee for the mention of their names. Most of the shops mentioned are reputable stores, but they are still paying for the mention of their name. Don't be fooled into thinking that these shops have the best prices or the finest products. They may, but then again, with careful shopping on your part, you may find a better bargain elsewhere.

MEDICAL FACILITY

Each ship will have a medical facility in case of injury or illness. A doctor and nurse are available 24 hours a day in case of an emergency.

The facility is not free except in case of a true emergency.

Having the doctor look at a mild sunburn or remove a splinter will cost you a flat fee on most ships. Aspirin and motion-discomfort pills are available at the Information Desk at no charge.

BEAUTY, HEALTH, FITNESS SPA/SALON

A haircut or a complete hair styling is available when the ship is at sea.

Each spa has its own menu of services offered (hair, nails, facials, massage, etc.), as well as sauna, showers, and exercise equipment. Some ships offer a complete list of beauty and exercise amenities while others offer a more limited variety. The Beauty Shop is usually a concession that is not owned by the cruiseship. The Beauty Shop Manager is in charge and will have a small but skilled staff at his or her disposal for your needs.

> *TIP: Reserve your hairstyling appointment early in the cruise since everyone wants to have his or her hair done for formal night! Massages fill up early. Since there may be only one masseuse or masseur, reserve early.*

LIBRARY

Most ships have a library that may double as a game room for cards or board games. The library contains books and magazines for a variety of tastes. You can check out a book or game at the beginning of the cruise and keep it until the final day if you wish. Remember, there is no mail delivery at sea, so it's impossible to have your favorite daily newspaper in the library. But then, getting away from it all is why you are probably taking this cruise! Local English language newspapers available at various ports may be purchased and placed in the library by the cruise staff.

GAME ROOM

This is a game room of coin-operated video games that are so popular with the younger set. Some cruise lines put these games in a separate room while others simply place them wherever they'll fit and not bother other passengers. What you should note is that almost all cruise lines have these games. They are a money maker for the cruise lines, and the kids love them! Children traveling with adults should be encouraged to use this room and not attempt to play the slot machines in the casino.

THE BRIDGE

This is where the Captain works.

It is located on one of the upper decks and in the front of the ship.

It's the navigational heart of the ship and is operational 24 hours a day, even when the ship is in port. However, like the cockpit of an airplane, you only visit the bridge when invited. Usually, once during the cruise there will be an opportunity to tour the bridge and gaze at all the hi-tech equipment that keeps the ship on an even keel. Most people are suprised that the wheel that steers the ship is one tenth the size that they imagined and that the ship has an automatic pilot control. Times have certainly changed since the days of the square rigger.

THE ENGINE ROOM

This is the area that produces power for the ship and keeps it moving.

It is located below the passenger and crew living quarters between the middle (mid-ships) and back end (aft) of the ship.

This area is usually off limits to passengers, for safety reasons more than anything else. On the older ships, the engine room tends to be a bit dirty, and it is very loud. Newer ships have engine rooms that look like operating rooms, white and very clean, but still loud . If you are interested enough, you will leave a note for the Chief Engineer and let him know of your interest to tour the engine room at his convenience. Most Chief Engineeers will go out of their way to accommodate you if at all possible. Just be ready to tour when given a time.

THE LAUNDRY ROOM

Located below the passenger living quarters.

It's a pretty busy place during the cruise and is almost always off limits to passengers unless you have a particularly valid reason to visit. It's very hot and noisy and, as we said, very busy. The laundry personnel wash and clean all passenger and crew clothing, not to mention the mountains of towels, napkins, linens, etc., week after week. The Laundry Manager is the person to contact if you want a tour, but don't get your hopes up!

THE GALLEY

Frequently referred to as the kitchen on most ships.

This is perhaps the busiest department on the ship before and during meals. All food that is prepared in separate areas (butcher shop, pastry shop, bakery, salad area, etc.) arrives here for cooking. It takes a small army of highly qualified individuals to prepare the daily menu for anywhere from 500 to 2,000 people and have it served hot and on time.

The Head Chef is in charge. The Sous-Chef is second in command.

Tours of the Galley are arranged during the cruise – during non-meal, quiet times, of course!

6

THE DINING ROOM

The dining room is perhaps the most popular of all the public rooms. It is most certainly the area of the most compliments.

Some ships have one main dining room while other large ships may have two or more, depending on size. Ships having more than one dining room may allow you to dine in the room you prefer. However, there are no guarantees; it's usually on a first-come, first-served basis. Some of the newer ships with multi-dining areas allow and even encourage guests to rotate dining rooms each evening.

YOUR SEATING ASSIGNMENT

You will be assigned to the dining room and a table based on the preferences that you gave your cruise consultant (smoking, non-smoking, early or late seating, table for two, window location). The Dining Room Manager or Maitre d' will do everything possible to fulfill your wishes. However, when the ship is filled to capacity, it can be difficult to grant every passenger exactly what he or she wants.

You will be assigned to a table that meets your smoking requirements. Be aware that the distinction between smoking and non-smoking areas may be no more than one table. (Many ships are now beginning to prohibit smoking altogether in their dining rooms).

Unless you are traveling with a group and request to be seated at the same table or close to each other, your dining companions are simply the luck of the draw. If you are uncomfortable at the table chosen for you, you can ask the Maitre d' to have you moved to another table. He or she will gladly do so, providing that there is space. Changes normally take a day to complete.

BREAKFAST

Breakfast in the dining room is always a treat.

The food is wonderful and nothing beats getting first-class service first thing in the morning.

Check out the egg dishes, and don't miss the array of pastries. Remember, this is not the week for diets! Most ships have a relaxed dress code for breakfast in the dining room. Shorts are almost always acceptable.

Breakfast in the dining room does not last all morning! Don't be disappointed by arriving too late. Check the times for breakfast in your cruise bulletin.

For those preferring a more casual breakfast (or for those who prefer to sleep-in), a buffet with grill is usually available outside or near the pool area. This allows you to have breakfast outdoors and in a more casual atmosphere. Bathing suits are permitted when eating indoors as long as they are covered with a cover-up or shirt.

And, for those who prefer to move at an even slower pace, you can order breakfast delivered to your cabin. Complete the cabin service breakfast form and place it outside your cabin door before retiring for the evening. Be sure to request a wake-up call from the front desk so that you'll be awake and ready to enjoy breakfast when it arrives.

LUNCH

On board a cruise ship, lunch can be as simple or as extravagant as you desire.

Eat a hot dog, hamburger, or barbeque ribs out by the pool. Or, if you prefer to be waited on in the dining room, slip into something comfortable (shorts are usually permitted in the dining room at lunchtime), and enjoy an open-seating (sit wherever you wish) atmosphere where you'll have your choice of everything from salad buffets to a full-course meal.

Of course, if the ship is in port, you can either return for lunch onboard or you can enjoy the local fare on shore at your own expense. The Tour Office can direct you to the most popular restaurants.

DINNER

This is the meal that everyone remembers. It's usually the high point of the day.

If the ship offers a First and a Second seating, you will have made your choice with your initial reservation. You will be seated by the Head Waiter (or Maitre d') on the first night. He or she will direct you to your assigned table. (Remember, your table number is on your boarding pass identification card.) You will now meet those passengers who have been assigned to the same table as you. These are the people you'll be dining with throughout the cruise, unless you request to be moved for some reason. Your table will be assigned to the same waiter and busboy for the entire cruise, and your Head Waiter (or Maitre d') will remain the same.

There are times when not every passenger gets the dining

room seating they request. Due to a number of factors, the dining room may be filled to capacity of either one of the seatings. Patience is strongly recommended. The first night at sea in the dining room can be confusing to some. Everyone is looking for his or her table, adjustments are being made to the new surroundings while everyone is getting to know each other. It simply is not the best time to request changes. See the Maitre d' after dinner and ask if he or she can possibly change your seating for the following evening. He or she will do everything possible to fullfill your wishes, but remember, he/she can't do the impossible. And, you may find that the seating you have been given turns out to be just fine.

FIRST (EARLY) SEATING:

If you are accustomed to eating between 5:00 P.M. and 7:00 P.M., we recommend that you choose First Seating.

The dining room opens at about 6:00 P.M., and you are finished with your meal in time to enjoy the evening shows and let the food settle, anticipating the midnight buffet.

SECOND (MAIN) SEATING:

If your lifestyle is such that you find yourself eating around 8:00 P.M. or later, then it will be wise for you to choose Second Seating.

This later meal time will allow you to relax during the early evening hours, take a nap, have a cocktail, or simply watch the sunset at sea.

The dining room opens at about 8:15 P.M. and you finish in time to relax and watch the late entertainment, visit the casino, or stroll about the deck and look at the stars.

> *TIP: The evening's entertainment is designed to accommodate those enjoying either first or second seating. So, don't worry about missing anything. All shows are presented for both dinner seatings.*

THE DINING ROOM MANAGER or THE MAITRE d'

He/She is in charge of the Dining Room.

He/She has complete responsibility for all Head Waiters, Waiters, Busboys, and any other personnel working in the dining room during meals.

Some ships which have more than one Dining Room may view them as separate restaurants and refer to the Dining Room Manager as The Maitre d' Hotel. The functions are similar, and it is the option of the cruise line to designate the title it prefers.

As of this writing, we have found both the Dining Room Manager and the Maitre' d positions to be filled predominently by males. There are some ships that employ women in these two positions as well as Head Waiter positions.

THE HEAD WAITER

There can be more than one Head Waiter; one for each section of the dining room.

Head Waiters are in charge of the waiters and busboys and are responsible for the dining room's operating smoothly.

The Head Waiter can solve any problems you may have or perform any number of services, from ordering special meals to preparing table-side flaming desserts. Your Head

Waiter will make himself/herself known to you on the first night and will see to it that he or she visits your table each evening to assure that all is satisfactory.

YOUR DINING ROOM WAITER/WAITRESS...

might also be referred to as the dining room Steward or Stewardess.

This is the person totally responsible for delivering the food to your table. He or she will take your order and can advise you on the preparation of a particular item on the menu. The waiter will normally have the responsibility of serving between 16 and 20 people at one seating. This is not unlike any large restaurant in the United States. A good waiter can set the tone for the table and interact with each table member in a manner that will add further enjoyment to the dining experience.

YOUR BUSBOY...

is sometimes referred to as the Assistant Dining Room Steward or Stewardess.

His or her responsibility is to ensure that all place settings are correct, that water is poured, that bread and butter, salt and pepper, sugar, etc. are all on the table. The Busboy will also have your iced tea or hot coffee delivered to the table exactly when and how you want it. He or she works in concert with the waiter and will see that attention is paid to you whenever the waiter is busy with someone else.

His or her future goal is to become a waiter or waitress.

We have found a few ships that do not use busboys. The waiter or waitress perform all functions for a fewer number of tables.

THE WINE STEWARD

Even if complimentary wine is offered with meals, the ship may have a Wine Steward on duty.

Many ships position the Wine Steward outside of the dining room as you first board the ship in order to acquaint you with the variety of wines and champagnes available. Many passengers will order wine for their evening meal at this time.

There can be two or more Wine Stewards per dining room. Your steward will introduce himself on the first night. At this time you can inform him that you enjoy a particular wine (from the wine list on your table) or that you are not interested in having wine with your meal. He will ask you how many glasses you would like (for you alone, you and whoever is traveling with you, or for the entire table – a nice gesture on your part). You will quickly learn if those at your table wish to share the wine with you. Often, a person or a couple at your table will reciprocate the following evening. Play it by ear, but don't feel embarrassed to order and enjoy your own wine with your meal. You are not expected to share it with others each night.

We have seen some cruise lines which utilize the Waiter or Waitress as a Wine Steward. Although this practice in no way deters from your enjoying a fine bottle of wine with your meal, be aware that many waiters do not have the time to devote to explaining the many wines available. They should, however, be able to recommend the proper wine that will complement the meal you choose.

> *TIP: If you do not finish your bottle of wine at one seating, ask the Wine Steward or your waiter to cork your bottle and mark it with your table number for enjoying it at dinner the following evening.*

THE MENU

The first thing you notice is that there are no prices. It's all paid for, so dig in!

The menu changes each day, except for breakfast, which will offer the same extensive variety each morning.

Both lunch and dinner offer a choice of appetizer, soup, pasta dish, main entree, and dessert.

The luncheon menu will offer a lighter fare with an array of salad dishes, sandwiches, etc.

Dinner is more elaborate, and you will always find beef, poultry, and fish at each meal.

The menu will specify items that are fat-free or lower in calories; and all selections are written in English. Many ships will have the menu translated into other languages (Spanish and German are most common) for non-English speaking guests.

The waiter will explain the contents of any dish that you are not familiar with, and you can feel free to order more than one entree if you care to. The waiter will gladly bring you a taste of any item on the menu. He'll see to it that the sauce is omitted from your potatoes, if you wish, or that you receive extra mint jelly with your lamb. Just ask!

Want two or three desserts? No problem. Just remember the rule of thumb: You'll gain one pound for each day. So wear your tightest clothes early in the cruise. They might not fit toward day six or seven!

SPECIAL REQUESTS

Given advanced notice, the chef can create any food dish within concept and cuisine.

Special diets, food restrictions, Kosher meals, etc. can all be arranged. Tell your cruise consultant when you make your reservation. Waiting until you arrive onboard may not be enough time to accommodate your wishes, especially if they require special foods and preparation.

BIRTHDAYS AND ANNIVERSARIES

Special-occasion cakes and songs to accompany them are part of the service.

Be sure to tell your waiter at least 24 hours before the occasion so that the chef can bake enough cakes and the waiters and busboys can tune up for your special serenade.

TYPICAL HOURS OF FOOD SERVICE

These will definitely vary from ship to ship. Dining times may differ, depending on whether or not your ship has relaxed hours of service and allows an open seating format for all meals.

Normally, meals are served within the following hours:

*Breakfast (Dining Room)	6:00 A.M. to 9:00 A.M.
*Breakfast Buffet	8:00 A.M. to 10:30 A.M.
*Lunch (dining Room)	12:00 Noon to 1:30 P.M.
*Luncheon Buffet	12:30 to 2:30 P.M.
*Afternoon Tea, Snacks, Ice Cream	4:00 P.M. to 5:00 P.M.
*Dinner (first seating)	6:00 P.M. to 7:30 P.M.
*Dinner (second seating)	8:15 P.M. to 9:45 P.M.
*Midnight Buffet	11:30 P.M. to 1:00 A.M.
*Cabin Service (Snacks)	24 hours a day (most ships)

> **TIP: Pay close attention to the listed times for meals whenever the ship is in port. Often, in order to accommodate those passengers departing for tours, breakfast, lunch and dinner are served earlier than normal.**

ORDERING BAR DRINKS DURING MEALS

No problem, except that the waiter or busboy can't bring them to you.

Anything from the bar, including seltzer water, soda, soft drinks, liquors, etc. must be delivered by a cocktail waiter or waitress. You will need to present your onboard charge card to pay for the drinks when delivered.

TIPPING (GRATUITIES)...

is often a misunderstood subject. All service personnel on the ship work for tips.

They are paid a base salary, guaranteed by the cruise line every month. That amount is complemented by the gratuities you give them in return for their service.

Waiters, busboys, bar personnel, cabin stewards, and the Maitre d' all work for tips. There is no hard-and-fast rule as to how much you should tip for a one-week cruise. The cruise line will present guidelines for what it believes to be fair. What you decide to give is a personal decision based on what you can afford and the quality of service you have received.

Tipping Guideline:

The suggested amount will vary from ship to ship.

What we show here is a range of tips, per person, per day or week.

Waiter	$2.00 - $3.50 per person per day
Busboy	$1.50 - $2.50 per person per day
Maitre d'	$5.00 per person for the week
Head Waiter	$5.00 per person for the week
Wine Steward	$1.00 for each bottle opened for you
Bartenders	Depending on the personal service received
Bar Waiters	Bar personnel receive an automatic 15% on every drink order they take. Tip extra if you believe they have earned it.
Cabin Stewards	$2.00 - $3.00 per person per day
Snack Stewards	$1.00 per delivery to your cabin

If you think that the person serving you has done more than is necessary to make your cruise pleasant, we believe that he or she should be rewarded. Even the most modest gratuity is appreciated.

Remember, you would pay quite a bit more in tips if you were eating similar meals in a nice restaurant back home. Actually, shipboard tipping guidelines are quite reasonable.

Tip an extra dollar or two to the cocktail waitress who knocks herself out serving your table of 10 in the lounge and never forgets what everyone is drinking. A dollar to the bartender who always remembers your name or your favorite drink shows that you appreciate his abilities.

Tip an extra $5.00 or more for a waiter or busboy if he made every meal an experience to remember and did more than you expected. Do the same for the cabin steward whom you rarely ever saw enter or exit your cabin and yet always kept it spotless!

Most cruise lines will deliver envelopes to your cabin on the second-to-last night, or provide them at the Purser's desk. These envelopes are used to hold cash tips for the Waiter, Busboy, and Cabin Steward.

Tip the Maitre d' and Head Waiter without using an envelope. Handing them cash is acceptable.

Bartenders, the Wine Steward and the Snack Stewards are usually tipped as the service is given. We have never seen a person turn down a deserved tip. Some cruise lines discourage tipping. Many cruise lines that cater to Europeans have the tips pre-paid. That's great, but the bottom line still seems to be — if the service is there, encourage it.

When in doubt, tip!

> *TIP: Don't get caught short at the end of the cruise. On the first day put away enough money to cover all basic tips for you and your party. It avoids embarrassment if you should have a bad night in the casino on your last night on board.*

7

ACTIVITIES ON BOARD

THE DAILY PROGRAM

Each day, you will receive a program (sometimes referred to as your daily bulletin) that lists the various events taking place on the ship. This program allows you to budget your time to those activies of interest to you. The daily program is printed and delivered to your cabin the evening before so that you can plan your day. It is also available at the Purser's Desk.

CRUISE STAFF

This is the staff that provides you with entertainment.

They not only sing and dance their way into your hearts, they also oversee the pool games, lectures, talent shows, religious services, contests, and other activities that allow you a brief escape from reality.

Activities provided by the cruise staff include:

* *BINGO*

This popular pastime may be held each day. Buy one or as many cards as you want. Some ships include a snowball-type Bingo where the grand prize increases (or snowballs) each day until some lucky guest wins (or shares) it all! We have seen some Bingo grand prizes exceed $2,000.00.

* LIP-SYNCH CONTEST

Care to imitate your favorite singer? Always want to roll your hips like Elvis, croon like Frank, be part of the Supremes, or look for "Where the Boys Are," like Connie? This is your golden opportunity. Lots of fun. Dress up and act the part, mouth the words, and let the magic of recorded tape do the rest. Great show!

* PASSENGER TALENT SHOW

No mouthing of words here. This is the real thing. Do you have a talent for telling jokes, singing, playing an instrument? This is your moment to entertain your fellow passengers with your particular (or peculiar) talent. Usually, this show is both touching and hilarious. You never know quite what to expect!

> **TIP:** *If you have a favorite song to sing and wish to participate in the talent show, bring the sheet music to that song if you have it. It will help the orchestra make you sound better.*

* HORSE RACES

Horseracing on the high seas! Passengers move the horses across the showroom track. The roll of the dice determines which of the six horses will move, and how far. Bet on the horse; win what the odds pay. You'll get caught up in the excitement from the very first race. Play the daily double that is held toward the end of the cruise. It could prove to be quite a nice payoff!

* COSTUME CONTEST

Bring your own costume or make it on board with materials supplied by the cruise staff. Some of the cos-

tumes are outrageous (as you can imagine). Keep it all in good taste, and have a lot of fun. Half the fun is deciding what to be!

* POOL GAMES

Dive for sunken treasure (spoons), toss water balloons, stuff your bikini with ping-pong balls, run around the pool with a tennis ball between your knees, identify your husband by feeling a lineup of male legs (while blindfolded) and any other crazy activity that the cruise staff can think up in order to keep you laughing and enjoying an hour of madness at poolside.

* MOVIES

Most ships show current films on your in-cabin television. Many ships are also showing current and classic films on the big screen during the day in the disco, theater or lounge. Some ships even serve popcorn.

* FITNESS AND SPORTS ACTIVITIES

More and more ships are taking fitness programs and activities very seriously. Most ships offer a varying number of early morning stretch programs, mile walks around the upper deck, step aerobics, low-impact aerobics, and an introduction to using the various pieces of gym equipment. You are allowed to choose the program that fits your particular exercise needs.

> **TIP:** *Even if you are not into a formal exercise program, a cruise is a great place to start. Pack some special clothes for exercise; gym shoes (sneakers), leotards, or gym shorts and T-shirt, any comfortable clothing you can wear during exercise.*

> *TIP: Learn a route from the pool to your cabin by the stairway and skip the elevators. Over a week's time, you'll get more exercise than you might imagine.*

* SPORT GAMES AND TOURNAMENTS

Some cruise lines are heavily involved in providing professional and amateur athletes in joining the passengers in various types of sport games from basketball to ping-pong tournaments. Many cruise lines operate sport-theme cruises with two or more professional athletes on board to discuss sports and actively participate in sporting activities. You may even get to meet NFL Hall-of-Fame great, and our good friend, Ray Nitschke and his lovely wife Jackie.

SHORE EXCURSIONS and TOURS

Shore tours are under the direction of the Shore Excursion Manager.

The Shore Excursion Manager is a member of the Cruise Staff and is responsible for everything from air-conditioned bus tours of major cities to reef snorkeling in crystal-clear ocean waters.

Many ships have itineraries that allow them to remain in port until early morning hours, some remaining over night. This allows you the opportunity to take a nightclub or late-night dinner tour in a group at a reasonable cost and in complete safety.

Tickets for the many tours are available at the Shore Excursion Desk and are announced in your daily bulletin.

SHOPPING

This is perhaps a major reason that you have decided to take a cruise, the shopping bargains in certain ports-of-call.

Your Cruise Staff will present a Travel and Shopping Lecture during your cruise. This talk will often include a guest lecturer who is very familiar with current shopping bargains in the port(s) you are to visit. This talk usually takes an hour and gives you many useful tips on how and where to purchase the best bargains.

Certain shops may be mentioned and even recommended by the Cruise Director. As said before, be aware that many of these shops pay a fee to the Cruise Staff for recommendation, and although they will be reputable establishments, they may not have the best prices in town. Comparison shop when looking for the best prices.

Each port that you visit will present its own unique shopping bargains. Some are better than others, depending on what you are looking for.

Bargains throughout the Caribbean are not as spectacular as they were ten years ago. Perfumes, electronics, cameras and watches all tend to be priced competitively among shops. The greatest saving is on taxes, especially on liquor and tobacco — items that are heavily taxed in the United States and Canada.

The shrewd shopper will know the price for a particular product back home, and will purchase accordingly.

Many times, uniqueness of a product is well worth the price simply because you would never be able to purchase anything like it back home, regardless of price. Artisan products that are seldom exported from Mexico, Alaska, or the Caribbean; unique liquors and local jewelry; carved items from woods or stone seldom seen outside of the region you are visiting. Rule of thumb: if you really fall in love with an item, buy it! You may never find another like it again.

On some ships the Cruise Staff will hold White Elephant Sales for those passengers who have second thoughts about a purchase and wish to put it up for sale, or exchange it for another item at this on-board, open flea market.

> **TIP:** *Don't wait until you are put under buying pressure and forget the foreign-exchange rate. Learn the exchange rate for local currency before you leave the ship. Practice converting local sums into dollars. Consider purchasing a low-cost electronic currency converter that will do the work for you.*

FORMAL PORTRAITS

Most ship photographers offer the opportunity to have formal photographs taken in a single photo or group photos. These are usually offered during a formal night prior to or immediately following dinner. This is an excellent opportunity to obtain a formal photograph of you and your family at a very competitive price. These portraits will be put on display and are available for purchase, as are all photographs taken by the ship's photographers during the cruise. On most ships, the photo gallery is open for viewing all day. Hours for purchasing photos are listed in the daily bulletin.

SINGLES' COCKTAIL PARTY

This event is offered early in the cruise to give unmarried passengers the opportunity to meet other singles of the same or opposite sex. It is a nice way to get to know others in a relaxed atmosphere before you meet again in the Disco.

REPEAT PASSENGER CLUB

Most Cruise Lines recognize those passengers who have

sailed with them before— either on this or other ships of their line. Usually, the Captain and members of his staff will host a private cocktail reception in honor of repeat passengers. On some ships, during port check-in, you will be asked to write down the number of times you have sailed with the cruise line. Other lines keep track by computer and provide you with special identification lapel pins and cards.

DAY CARE PROGRAMS

During school vacation months many ships employ a Youth Counselor or a member of the Cruise Staff to conduct a youth program onboard. Much like a day camp, young people are offered activities by age. These give the parents an opportunity to spend some free time on board without having to entertain their offspring.

WINE TASTING

Spend an hour learning about the unique tastes of the fine wines served on board the ship. Many ships will allow you a discount if you purchase a bottle of these wines during your meal, providing that you've attended the Wine Tasting Seminar.

PERFUME TESTING

The Gift Shop will hold a perfume seminar where you can test the various fragrances sold on board and learn more about each. Although this session seems to be more popular with the women on board, many men attend as well. Learn what is currently popular with the ladies!

FASHION SHOWS

Let the Gift Shop and Cruise Staff model the fashions available for sale in ship's boutiques. It's a good opportunity to determine how an item looks off the rack and which combinations go well together. A great opportunity for determining gift ideas, it's an interesting and worthwhile session for both women and men.

GRANDPARENT BRAGGING TIME

Got grandchildren? Bring photos and stories about each. Share them with equally proud grandma and grandpa travelers. Some of the stories you'll hear will bring a tear to your eye, or keep you laughing for hours

THEME DINNER NIGHTS

Many ships will arrange one or more dinners around a theme, a country, or a port the ship is visiting. Quite often the midnight buffet will be presented as a theme as well. Ships traveling to Mexico will often conduct a Mexican Buffet. In the Caribbean it is a Caribbean Night. Other ships may offer a Western Bar-B-Q or a County Fair with games included. The ideas go on and on.

> *TIP: Pack an open-collar Hawaiian-type shirt and a pair of comfortable cotton slacks or skirt for enjoying the Caribbean or Mexican theme nights, jeans, boots and hat for Western night, and '50s garb for the '50s/'60s Rock n' Roll party. Many ships will adjust the dress code and encourage passengers to dress in keeping with the theme.*

8

PORTS OF CALL

The following will give you an idea of the basic itineraries of most cruise lines.

Seven-day cruises offer a wide range of ports of call. We have listed the ports most commonly visited for quick reference only. Check with your Cruise Consultant for current itineraries:

1.) CARIBBEAN (Year-Round)

    1-Day - Ft. Lauderdale and Miami to:
- The Bahamas
- Cruise to nowhere

    1-Day - Tampa to:
- Cruise to nowhere

    3-4 Day - Ft. Lauderdale, Cape Canaveral, and Miami to:
- The Bahamas
- Key West
- Cozumel, Mexico

    7-Day - Ft. Lauderdale and Miami to:

        EASTERN CARIBBEAN
- San Juan
- St. Thomas
- St. Maarten
- Nassau, Bahamas

WESTERN CARIBBEAN

- Cozumel, Mexico
- Grand Cayman
- Jamaica
- Nassau, Bahamas

7-Day - San Juan to:

SOUTHERN CARIBBEAN

- Barbados
- Martinique
- St. Lucia
- Antigua
- St. Thomas
- St. Martin
- Aruba

New ports are being served by ships sailing out of Aruba and Montego Bay, Jamaica. See your local Travel Agent's Cruise Consultant for further information.

2.) MEXICO (Year-Round)   (Western Coast)

3-4 Day - Los Angeles to:
- Catalina Island
- Ensenada, Mexico
- San Diego

7- Day - Los Angeles to:

MEXICAN RIVIERA
- Cabo San Lucas
- Mazatlan
- Puerta Vallarta
- Acapulco

3.) HAWAII   (Year-Round)

3, 4, and 7 Day - Honolulu and the Islands

4.) ALASKA (May to October)

7-Day - Vancouver B.C. to Anchorage
Anchorage to Vancouver

5.) BERMUDA (May to October)

7-Day - New York City to Bermuda

6.) NEW ENGLAND (May to October)

7-Day - New York City to Montreal
Montreal to New York City
- Newport R.I.
- Cape Cod Canal
- Provincetown, MA
- Boston
- Bar Harbor, ME
- Sydney, P.E.I.
- Halifax, N.S.
- St.Johns, N.S.

9

PRACTICAL ADVICE

FOREIGN CURRENCY

Don't worry about exchanging your dollars before you leave home.

All countries in the Bahamas and Caribbean and Mexico will accept U.S. dollars in exchange for goods. Larger shops will accept travelers' checks. Most shops will take major credit cards, especially MasterCard and Visa.

We have found that more and more of the smaller stores in Mexico are adding anywhere from 4 to 6 per cent onto your purchase if you use credit cards of any kind.

In foreign ports your overall bargaining and purchasing power is much higher if you use cash.

LANGUAGE

English is spoken in the majority of countries in the Caribbean.

You will find that many people in Mexico speak some English.

Taxi drivers, waiters, store clerks, and street vendors speak enough English to conduct business.

All major retail shops have personnel who are completely bilingual.

> ***TIP: When visiting Spanish-speaking countries, your ability to speak a few words in Spanish will go a long way in creating a positive relationship and perhaps encouraging improved service. It shows respect for their language and a willingness to communicate as best you can.***

LUGGAGE

Soft-sided and slim-profile luggage works best since it will fit under your bed and give you extra closet space. The more luggage you bring on board, the more luggage you'll have to store in your cabin.

CHECKLIST OF THINGS TO BRING WITH YOU

The following is a list of handy items that you might wish to consider bringing with you. Not every item on the list will be applicable to your particular cruise, and sundry items can be found in the ship's gift shop:

Camera
Extra camera batteries/flash batteries (if an unusual size)
Portable alarm clock
Skin cream
Sunscreen Lotion
Extra pair of contact lens or eyeglasses
Contact lens cleaning/rewetting drops
Personal prescription medication
Antacids (particular brand)
Aspirin (particular brand)
Pill containers
Small plastic bottles for liquids (skin cleaner, after shave, etc.)
Zip lock bags for liquids and liquid purchases
Good walking shoes
Comfortable sun hat

Lip Balm
Sunglasses
Gym exercise clothes
Eye covers (for mid-day naps)
Photographs of children/grandchildren
Theme Night clothes
    (Mexican, Caribbean, Western, '50s & '60s)
Light sweater
Extension cord
Canvas shopping bag (available in most gift shops)
Extra soft suitcase or zipper bag (for gift purchases)
Portable iron or clothes steamer
    (ships provide a total laundry service)
A good book
Magazine articles that you have not yet had time to read

WHAT NOT TO BRING:

Work
Problems
A Negative Attitude

A CRUISE VOCABULARY
(that will make you sound like you know what you are talking about)

ACCOMMODATION: This is your room – otherwise known as your CABIN.

AFT: Near, toward or at the rear of the ship – otherwise known as the STERN.

CATEGORY: The price grades of cabins from the most to least expensive.

DEBARKATION: Leaving the ship – getting off the ship.

DECK: The floor. Also used in reference to the various levels (or floors) on a ship.

DECK PLAN: An overhead layout of the ship, deck by deck.

EMBARKATION: Entering the ship – boarding or getting on the ship.

FATHOM: Measurement of water depth – equal to 6 feet.

FORWARD: Near, toward or at the front of the ship – otherwise known as the BOW.

FREE PORT: A port or place free of customs duty and most customs regulations.

INSIDE CABIN: A cabin having no windows or portholes.

KNOT: A unit of speed equal to 1 nautical mile per hour (6,080.2 feet) as compared to a land mile of 5,280 feet.

MIDSHIPS: In or toward the middle of the ship.

OPEN SEATING: Free access to unoccupied tables in the dining room — sit wherever you like.

OPTION: Cruise line's offering of a particular cabin for a specified period of time during which the passenger decides whether or not to accept. Acceptance is confirmed by a deposit or final payment.

PORT: The left side of the ship when facing the bow. Identified by red lights on that side. (Remember, Port wine is red.) Also used to describe a stop on the ship's itinerary.

SHIP REGISTRY: The country under whose laws the ship and its owners are obliged to comply, in addition to compliance with the laws of the countries at which the ship calls in its itinerary.

STARBORD: The right side of the ship when facing the bow. Identified by green lights on that side.

STATEROOM: Your cabin.

TENDER: A small boat used to move passengers to and from the ship and shore when not in port.

WATERLINE: The line at the side of the ship's hull which corresponds with the surface of the water.

HMS: Her Majesty's Ship
MS: Motor Ship
MTS: Motor Turbine Ship
MV: Motor Vessel
RMS: Royal Mail Ship
SS: Steamship
SSC: Semi Submergible Craft
TSS: Turbine Steam Ship
USS: United States Ship (U.S. Navy)

LIST OF CURRENT CRUISE SHIPS

COMPANY	SHIP	YEAR BUILT	# OF PASSENGERS
AMERICAN HAWAII CRUISES	Constitution	1951	778
	Independence	1950	752
CARNIVAL CRUISE LINES	Ecstasy	1991	2040
	Fantasy	1990	2040
	Sensation	1993	2040
	Fascination	1994	2040
	Imagination	1995	2040
	Jubilee	1986	1500
	Celebration	1987	1486
	Holiday	1985	1452
	Festivale	1961	1148
	Tropicale	1981	1022
CELEBRITY CRUISE LINES	Horizon	1990	1354
	Zenith	1992	1354
	Meridian	1963	1106
	Century	1995	TBA
CLUB MED SALES	Club Med I	1989	386
	Club Med II	1992	386
CLIPPER CRUISE LINE	Yorktown Clipper	1988	148
	Nantucket Clipper	1984	102
	Society Explorer	1969	102
COMMODORE CRUISE LINE	Enchanted Seas	1958	726
	Enchanted Isle	1958	726

COSTA CRUISE LINE		CostaClassica	1991	1300
		CostaRomantica	1993	1300
		CostaMarina	1990	772
		CostaAllegra	1992	772
CUNARD CROWN CRUISES				
		Crown Dynasty	1993	830
		Crown Jewel	1992	830
		Crown Monarch	1990	550
		Cunard Princess	1977	805
		Cunard Countess	1976	790
CRYSTAL CRUISES		Crystal Harmony	1990	960
		Crystal Symphony	1994	960
CUNARD LINE		Queen Elizabeth II	1969	1814
		Vistafjord	1973	736
		Sagafjord	1965	589
		Sea Goddess I	1984	116
		Sea Goddess II	1985	116
DELTA QUEEN STEAMBOAT COMPANY		American Queen	1995	412
		Mississippi Queen	1976	404
		Delta Queen	1926	176
DIAMOND CRUISE		Radisson Diamond	1992	354
DISCOVERY CRUISE LINE		Discovery I	1970	1250
		(One day cruises only)		
DOLPHIN CRUISE LINE		Sea Breeze I	1956	840
		Ocean Breeze	1955	732
		Dolphin IV	1956	588

FANTASY CRUISE LINE	Britanis	1932	926
	Amerikanis	1952	609
GOLD STAR CRUISES	Star of Texas	1961	906
			(One day cruises only)
			(monthly 3-day Mexican cruise)
HOLLAND AMERICA LINE	Statendam	1992	1627
	Westerdam	1986	1494
	Ryndam	1994	1266
	Maasdam	1993	1266
	Niew Amsterdam	1983	1214
	Noordam	1984	1214
	Rotterdam	1959	1114
MAJESTY CRUISE LINE	Royal Majesty	1992	1056
NORWEGIAN CRUISE LINE	Norway	1960	2044
	Seaward	1988	1534
	Dreamward	1992	1260
	Windward	1993	1260
	Starward	1968	778
	Southward	1971	774
PALM BEACH CRUISE LINE	Viking Princess	1964	366
PREMIER CRUISE LINE	Starship Oceanic	1965	1138
	Starship Atlantis	1982	972
	Starship Majestic	1972	764

PRINCESS CRUISE LINE	Sun Princess	1995	1950
	Crown Princess	1990	1590
	Regal Princess	1991	1590
	Star Princess	1989	1470
	Sky Princess	1984	1212
	Royal Princess	1984	1200
	Fair Princess	1956	906
	Golden Princess	1972	830
	Island Princess	1971	624
	Pacific Princess	1971	624
REGENCY CRUISES	Regent Sky	1995	1000
	Regent Rainbow	1958	960
	Regent Star	1957	974
	Regent Sun	1964	816
	Regent Sea	1957	712
	Regent Jewel	1967	500
	Regent Spirit	1962	400
RENAISSANCE CRUISES	Renaissance I–IV	1989-90	100
	Renaissance V–VIII	1991-92	114
ROYAL CARIBBEAN CRUISE LINE	Sovereign of the Seas	1987	2392
	Majesty of the Seas	1992	2354
	Monarch of the Seas	1991	2354
	Legend of the Seas	1995	1600
	Nordic Empress	1990	1610
	Viking Serenade	1982	1514
	Song of America	1982	1414
	Nordic Prince	1971	1038
	Song of Norway	1970	1022
	Sun Viking	1972	728
ROYAL CRUISE LINE	Crown Odyssey	1988	1052
	Star Odyssey	1972	829
	Royal Odyssey	1973	765

ROYAL VIKING LINE	Royal Viking Queen	1992	212
	(Will sail as the Queen Odyssey beginning Jan'95 for Royal Cruise Line.)		
	Royal Viking Sun	1988	740
	(Has been purchased by Cunard).		
SEA ESCAPE LTD	Scandanavian Dawn	1968	1050
			(One day cruises only)
SEAWIND CRUISE LINE	Seawind Crown	1961	654
SEABOURN CRUISE LINE	Seabourn Pride	1988	212
	Seabourn Spirit	1989	212
SILVERSEA CRUISES	Silver Cloud	1994	296
	Silver Wind	1995	296
SUN LINE CRUISES	Stella Maris	1960	180
	Stella Oceanis	1965	300
	Stella Solaris	1953	620
WINDSTAR CRUISES	Wind Song	1987	148
	Wind Spirit	1988	148
	Wind Star	1986	148
WORLD EXPLORER CRUISES	Universe	1953	540

INDEX

ACTIVE OR QUIET CRUISE	8
ACTIVITIES ON BOARD	65
AIR/SEA PACKAGE	14
AIRPORT	33
ALASKA	77
ALONE— A CABIN FOR MYSELF	24
ARRIVAL AT THE PIER	34
BAR DRINKS DURING MEALS	60
BARS	43
BEAUTY, HEALTH, FITNESS SPA	46
BERMUDA	77
BINGO	65
BIRTHDAYS AND ANNIVERSARIES	59
BOARDING PASS	36
BREAKFAST	52
BRIDGE	47
BUSBOY	56
CABIN LOCATION	21
CABIN STEWARD	38
CABINS FOR THE PHYSICALLY CHALLENGED	25
CANCEL MY CRUISE	17
CARIBBEAN	75
CARRY-ON LUGGAGE	34
CASH ONBOARD THE SHIP	28
CASINO	44
CHECKLIST OF THINGS TO BRING WITH YOU	80
CHOOSING YOUR FIRST CRUISE	1
CLOTHES	29
COSTUME CONTEST	66
CREDIT CARDS ONBOARD THE SHIP	27
CRUISE CANCELLATION INSURANCE	18
CRUISE ONLY RATE	15
CRUISE SHIP VOCABULARY	81

CRUISE STAFF	65
DAILY PROGRAM/BULLETIN	65
DAY CARE PROGRAMS	72
DINING ROOM MANAGER	55
DINING ROOM WAITER	56
DINNER	53
DISCO	43
DISCOUNT ON MY CRUISE	13
DOCTOR	32
DOCUMENTS	35
ENGINE ROOM	47
FARES	13
FASHION SHOWS	72
FEATURES	22
FIRST (EARLY) SEATING	54
FITNESS AND SPORTS ACTIVITIES	67
FOREIGN CURRENCY	79
FORMAL CLOTHES	31
FROM YOUR HOME TO YOUR CABIN	27
GALLEY	48
GAME ROOM	47
GETTING TO THE SHIP	33
GIFT SHOPS	44
GRANDPARENT BRAGGING TIME	73
GROUP RATE	14
HAWAII	76
HEAD WAITER	55
HORSE RACES	66
INFORMATION DESK	41
INSURANCE ON MY LUGGAGE	19
LANGUAGE	79
LARGE SHIP	4
LAUNDRY ROOM	48
LEAVE A DAY EARLY	16
LIBRARY	46
LIFE BOAT DRILL	39
LIP SYNCH CONTEST	66
LUGGAGE	80
LUNCH	53
MAKING YOUR CRUISE RESERVATIONS	11
MANY PORTS or MORE SEA TIME	7
MEDICAL FACILITY	45

MEDIUM SHIP	5
MEETING ROOMS	43
MEGA SHIP	4
MENU	58
MEXICO	76
MOVIES	67
NEW ENGLAND	77
OLDER SHIP vs NEW SHIP	5
PASSENGER TALENT SHOW	66
PERFUME TESTING	72
PERSONAL DOCUMENTS	27
PETS	33
PHOTOGRAPHER	36
POOL GAMES	67
PORT CHARGES	16
PORTRAITS	71
PORTS OF CALL	75
PRACTICAL ADVICE	79
REFUND	17
REPEAT PASSENGER CLUB	71
SEATING ASSIGNMENT	51
SECOND (MAIN) SEATING	54
SHIP SIZE	4
SHOPPING	69
SHORE EXCURSIONS and TOURS	68
SHOTS OR VACCINATIONS	32
SHOW LOUNGES	42
SINGLES COCKTAIL PARTY	71
SMALL SHIP	5
SPECIAL REQUESTS	58
SPECIALISTS	12
SPORT GAMES AND TOURNAMENTS	68
STAY A DAY OR TWO AFTER THE CRUISE?	16
SUITE	23
TAKING A TOUR OF THE SHIP	41
THE DINING ROOM	51
THE MAITRE d'	55
THEME CRUISES	7
THEME DINNER NIGHTS	73
THREE OR FOUR PEOPLE IN A CABIN	24
TIP THE PORTERS	35
TIPPING (GRATUITIES)	60

TOUR DESK	42
TRAVEL AGENCY	11
TRAVEL AGENT	11
TRAVELERS CHECKS	28
TYPES OF CABINS	21
TYPICAL HOURS OF FOOD SERVICE	59
VISITORS ON BOARD	37
WEAR DURING THE DAY	30
WEAR WHEN GOING ASHORE	30
WHAT HAPPENS TO MY LUGGAGE	33
WHAT HAPPENS WHEN I CHECK IN AT THE PIER	36
WHAT HAPPENS WHEN I STEP ON BOARD	37
WHAT NOT TO BRING	81
WINE STEWARD	57
WINE TASTING	72

THANK YOU FOR PURCHASING THIS BOOK.

WE HOPE IT HAS HELPED YOU PLAN AND ENJOY YOUR CRUISE.

Needless-to-say, we could not cover each and every aspect of the ideal cruise vacation. We realize that you may have observed an area that we failed to mention.

If so, please remove this page and mail it to us with your comments.

Include information and tips you believe we should have included in this book. If your suggestion is accepted, we will include it in a future edition. And we'll even credit your suggestion if you'd like!

Thanks in advance for helping to make **CHOOSING THE RIGHT CRUISE FOR YOU** a complete and up-to-date publication dedicated to helping the first-time and experienced cruiser plan and enjoy the cruise of a lifetime!

• • • • •

YES, I would like to offer the following information that I believe should be included in future editions of **CHOOSING THE RIGHT CRUISE FOR YOU:**

```
┌─────────────────────────────────────────┐
│                                         │
│                                         │
│                                         │
│                                         │
└─────────────────────────────────────────┘
```

NAME:

ADDRESS:

CITY: STATE: ZIP:

MAIL TO: A BON VOYAGE GUIDE
          CHOOSING THE RIGHT CRUISE FOR YOU.
          C/O DISTINCTIVE PUBLISHING CORP.
          P.O. BOX 17868
          PLANTATION, FL 33318-7868

**SPECIAL OFFER FOR
TRAVEL AGENTS AND CRUISE LINES
ONLY!!**

We will run a special promotional printing
for your business to include
COMPLIMENTS OF YOUR BUSINESS
on the front cover. Please call for details.

Aditional copies of
CHOOSING THE RIGHT CRUISE FOR YOU
by John Wm. Macchi and Art Kane,
may be ordered by sending a check or
money order for $ 12.95 postpaid for
each copy to:

Distinctive Publishing Corp.
P.O. Box 17868
Plantation, FL 33318-7868
(305)975-2413

Quantity discounts are also available
from the publisher

ABOUT THE ILLUSTRATOR

Jill Pabich is a freelance illustrator and decorative painter. She is a graduate of the Boston Museum School and Tufts University, where she majored in Fine Arts with emphasis on painting and drawing. She presently resides in Jamaica Plain, Massachusetts and is currently at work illustrating a book for children.

HM847-TN
40